Another creative book
from **The Brothers**

THANK YOU!

This book has been inspired by our sons and family.

It was created with a lot of love and joy.

It is very important to us to hear what you think about it.

Please click the link below and leave a review

or send us an email : the.kids.books.4u@gmail.com.

Lots of love for you and your family

If there are errors, or anything you would like to see changed, please email us at :
the.kids.books.4u@gmail.com
You can also visit Leo Super Hero Site
We answer every email.
Don't forget to rate.

Thank you for your time and happy reading!
Yours,
TheBrothers

A free gift is waiting for your kids at the end of the book

This is Leo. Leo is seven years old and he lives in a two- story house with his parents, his younger sister and Milkshake the cat. Leo is a superhero and he has a superhero outfit that his mom made for him.

It's Sunday morning. Everyone is fast asleep. Well, not exactly everyone, because someone in creeping up to Leo's room… it's Milkshake the cat.

Milkshake pushes the door open and enters the room. She walks up to Leo's bed, jumps up onto it and comes close to Leo's face. She starts licking Leo's face. "Milkshake, why are you waking me up, what is it?" Milkshake continues to lick Leo's face. Leo realizes that she wants to show him something.

Leo gets up, goes to his closet, opens up the closet and takes out his superhero outfit.

His superhero outfit includes Lego gloves, a motorcycle helmet and a baseball bat. Leo takes his outfit out, puts it on and says to Milkshake "Come on Milkshake, lead the way, I'm right behind you".

Leo and Milkshake go downstairs quietly, not to wake anyone. Leo follows
Milkshake who leads him towards the kitchen.

Leo and Milkshake enter the kitchen, and suddenly she stops in the corner. Leo looks carefully and sees a hole in the wall. "Is that what you wanted to show me?" Leo asks Milkshake.

Leo bends down and tries to peep into the hole. It is dark. Leo can't see a thing. He looks around to see if there's something he can use to shine light into the hole. Leo notices his mother's hand mirror on the kitchen table and thinks to himself that by using sunlight and the mirror, he might be able to shine light into the hole.

Leo uses the mirror and the sunlight coming in from the kitchen window and slowly shines light into the hole.

Inside the hole he suddenly notices a little gray mouse. "How did this little mouse get here?" he wonders. "Milkshake, do you know how this little mouse got here?"

Suddenly Milkshake pulls on Leo's superhero outfit and leads him to the yard. In the yard, behind the bushes, Leo sees a family of mice. He can see that one mouse is running around, as if it is looking for something. It has lost something.

"Well done", Leo says to Milkshake. "Now we should take the mouse back to its family. But how can we get the scared little mouse to come out of its hole?"

"I have an idea!" Leo shouts as he runs up the stairs to his room. There, in his room, he picks up a few Lego blocks and runs back down. He opens the refrigerator, takes out some cheese and takes a box of breakfast cereal from the cupboard.

Leo walks up to the hole in the wall and builds a kind of maze, and at the end of the maze he puts the cheese.

He waits….and waits…and waits.

"Patience, Milkshake, patience. It will all work out eventually," he whispers to Milkshake.

All of a sudden… a tiny nose comes peeping out of the hole, then two eyes and a little gray body. It seems that the mouse is heading out towards the cheese. "Let's wait until it comes out, and using the box, we can take it to its family" Leo whispers to Milkshake. They wait patiently and the mouse goes on and on and snap! Leo catches the mouse inside the cereal box.

Leo and Milkshake run outside. They're in a hurry. They have a mouse in a cereal box and they want to release it as fast as possible.

Leo and Milkshake run to the yard where, by the bushes, they see the family of mice that they saw earlier. Leo gently puts the cereal box on the ground and releases the mouse. "It looks like they're hugging," Leo says to Milkshake.

Leo Superhero feels happy. He feels that he has done a good deed in helping the mouse to find its family. He turns to go back into the house, but he can feel Milkshake pulling on his superhero outfit, not letting him leave just yet.

Milkshake goes to the cereal box, takes out the cheese and gives it to Leo. "Well done Milkshake. Well done." Leo breaks the cheese into small pieces and puts them on the grass. The happy mice skitter towards the cheese, grab it and vanish into the backyard bushes.

"I think we did a good deed today, and it's time to go to bed," Leo says to Milkshake as they go back up to his room. After all…it's Sunday morning…and everyone is still asleep.

THE END

(What do you want to be ? Look at the next page)

I WANNA BE
A FIREFIGHTER

Another creative book from The Brothers

I Wanna Be a FireFighter is our new Book.

A Great motivation & Education Book.

Include Great Facts & Illustrations

Now On Amazon

Click Here

LEO - SUPERHERO
A SUNDAY MORNING ADVENTURE

FIND THE FIVE DIFFERENCES IN THE PICTURES

LEO - SUPERHERO

A SUNDAY MORNING ADVENTURE

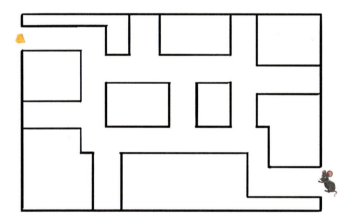

HELP THE MOUSE TO FIND THE RIGHT WAY TO THE CHEESE

ABOUT US

"As parents we have encountered quite a few questions and our children's thirst for knowledge and their need to receive answers to their questions - right here and right now. We have put our experience in inventing stories and storytelling to use. We pour heaps of imagination into our stories and most importantly we provide the children with the correct tools to deal with the day-to-day issues of the world. This is the reason that we write these books, we want the children, ours and yours, to explore, to be able to cope and to make use of knowledge, tools and wisdom to solve problems and cope in our world."

Leo's Sunday Adventure begins early one Sunday morning when everybody is asleep. His cat, Milkshake, wakes him up and leads him to the kitchen where he finds something special. This is the beginning of Leo and Milkshake's short adventure in the house and the back yard. This is a wonderful story for children.
The story teaches children the importance of patience and love of others (they will meet a cat that does not always chase mice) and they will learn how Leo improvises, creatively using objects that he has learnt about.

For any comments remarks or special requets send us an email :
The.kids.books.4u@gmail.com

Made in the USA
Middletown, DE
23 February 2015